ALL SORTS OF
SORTS

Word Sorts That Reinforce
Spelling and Phonetic Patterns

by Sheron Brown

A Teaching Resource Center Publication

Published by
Teaching Resource Center

14525 SW Millikan, #11910 Beaverton, OR 97005-2343
1-800-833-3389
www.trcabc.com

Edited by Anne Linehan and Laura Woodard
Design & production by Janis Poe

PRINTED IN THE UNITED STATES OF AMERICA ISBN: 1-56785-049-9

Table of Contents

Short Vowel Phonogram Sorts

* from Wylie and Durrell's list

Blend Sorts

Digraph Sorts

Plural and Ending Sorts

Contractions and Compound Words

Long Vowel Phonogram Sorts

* from Wylie and Durrell's list

R-Controlled Vowel Sorts

Long Vowel Pattern Sorts

Introduction

A Guide for Using Word Sorts in the Classroom

The word sorts in this book will give your students opportunities to practice and reinforce their word work in a very fun and different format. They'll learn to sort groups of words according to characteristics such as spelling, meaning, endings, sound patterns, and other shared properties. The various word sorts can be done as individual, small group, or whole class activities. All you need to make it happen is this book, a copy machine and scissors! The sorts are designed so that you can use them as either open sorts or closed sorts. In **closed sorts,** students sort the words by specific characteristics that have been predefined by the teacher. In **open sorts,** students discover and identify the characteristics of a group of words they have been given. How they choose to group the words is entirely up to them!

There are almost as many types of word sorts as there are words. At the lower primary levels, students may sort words by the number of letters in each word or perhaps by beginning or ending sounds. As their knowledge of words increases, the sorting possibilities increase as well. They may begin to sort by prefixes, suffixes, vowels, phonograms, roots, spelling rules, number of syllables and word meaning. Whatever skills or concepts you are teaching your students in any curricular area could conceivably be turned into a word sort!

A note about the phonograms: The phonogram sorts in this book include the thirty-seven high frequency phonograms identified by educational researchers Richard E. Wylie and Donald D. Durrell in 1970. Knowing these and other important phonograms will enable students to unlock hundreds of words. The Wylie and Durrell phonograms are marked with an asterisk (*) in the Table of Contents.

- Word sorts enable students to attend to the actual structure of words in print as they carefully scrutinize the letters and patterns in each word to determine how to catego-

Why do word sorts?

rize it.
- Students learn classification skills as they discover how sets of words they are given might be alike.
- Word sorts allow a teacher to assess each student's understanding of the many phonetic, spelling and word identification strategies being taught in the classroom.
- Word sorts are easy-to-check assessment tools that enable a teacher to quickly evaluate a student's understanding of a strategy without resorting to the usual paper and pencil test format.
- Word sorts provide a multi-sensory experience as students read, sort, manipulate and categorize words in multiple ways.
- Word sorts allow students to look at words from their various levels of knowledge about how words work.
- Students are able to apply their knowledge about how words work in an organized, yet pleasing and fun format.
- Students are empowered to make their own decisions about word categories based on their personal knowledge of words.

1. Start with the first section of the book and select words that the class, group, or individual can read. **Students cannot be expected to sort a group of words if they cannot read them.** Teach word sorting with an *open sort* first by presenting the students with short, easy, two- and

three-letter words. Instruct the students to cut apart the word sort cards and organize them however they want. When all students have finished their sorts, have volunteers share how they decided to organize the words. Be accepting of all categories students share as they explain how they sorted their word cards, as this is what *open sort* means.

Modeling the Word Sorts

2. After students are comfortable with an open sort and what is involved in word sorting, present them with a *closed sort.* Demonstrate how to place the two category names at the top of their desks or tables. Show the students how to look carefully at each word card to see which of the two categories each word will fit under. Teach the students to check all of the words under each category to ensure that each word placed there shares the common characteristic of that category.

3. Have the students mix up the word cards and re-sort them under the given categories.

4. If students are ready, have them mix up the word cards again and do a *speed sort* where they race against the clock. Have students raise their hands when they have completed and checked their word sorts. Write the time it took the class, group, or fastest individual to sort the cards on the board. Repeat the sort and challenge the students to beat the time posted. This is a fun way to have students read and re-read the word sort cards as they furiously sort them into the given categories.

5. After students are comfortable with the procedures of word sorting, introduce another *closed sort,* but this time include two or three words that will not fit under the given categories. Model selecting one of the **OUT OF SORTS** words and demonstrate how this particular word will not fit under any of the categories. **OUT OF SORTS** words should be placed in their own category.

6. After students have had enough practice doing both *open* and *closed* two-category sorts along with **OUT OF SORTS** words, introduce a third word sort category and then a fourth. Gradually increase the number of categories as your students become more and more comfortable with

doing word sorts.

7. Teaching your students to do a *blind sort* will help them sharpen their auditory discrimination skills. Have them write the names of two or three word sort categories on blank word sort cards, for example short *a* words, long *a* words, and long *e* words. Call out the words and have the students either point to or say the name of the sort category where it goes. Blind sorts are particularly useful when you want to focus on the sound patterns in a set of words as opposed to the visual patterns.

8. A *writing sort* focuses on both auditory and visual patterns in words and is a combination of a closed and open sort. Provide the students with key words to use as column headers as well as spelling guides. Call out the words and have the students write them on blank word cards (page 166) and place them under the key words. After all of the words are dictated and sorted, share the correct word sort either on the overhead or on the board in order for students to check their spelling and sorting and make corrections.

9. When selecting words and/or word sort categories for your students, make sure you have taught the word features or concepts before asking students to sort the words. This is important when you have them sort words by meaning. Make sure abstract concepts are clear to them before they sort by characteristics such as *living* and *non-living.*

1. **open sort** – The teacher provides only the words, and the students decide the sort categories based on what they see. Open sorts are valuable as they provide a window for the teacher into each student's word work and which features they are noticing or not noticing.

2. **closed sort** – The teacher provides the categories for the word sort. Closed sorts are used more frequently than open sorts, as they allow

- For an *open sort,* copy only the words below the dotted line, and let the students use the extra strips of paper from the sides to create their own category cards.

- For a *closed sort,* make copies of the entire word sort

Glossary of Word Sort Terms

1. **open sort** – The teacher provides only the words, and the students decide the sort categories based on what they see. Open sorts are valuable as they provide a window for the teacher into each student's word work and which features they are noticing or not noticing.

2. **closed sort** – The teacher provides the categories for the word sort. Closed sorts are used more frequently than open sorts, as they allow the teacher to focus students' attention on a word feature, characteristic or pattern the class is currently studying. Closed sorts are also valuable assessment tools. The teacher can rapidly assess student understanding of word features by simply checking the students' sorts against the Answer Keys (pages 170-189).

3. **speed sort** – This is usually a timed sort that students can do once they are adept at sorting words. Speed sorts are excellent for building fluency and accuracy when working with known patterns and concepts. Students can record the time it takes to sort a given set of words and then try to beat their records.

4. **blind sort** – This is a closed sort in which the teacher calls out the words and the students point to or say the categories they see listed on the worksheet or written on the board or overhead. Blind sorts are particularly useful when the teacher wants to focus on the sound patterns rather than the visual patterns of the words.

5. **writing sort** – The students have key words, provided by the teacher, written as column headers. They write words under the appropriate categories as the teacher calls them out, using the key words as spelling guides. Writing sorts focus on both auditory and visual patterns in words and are a combination of closed and blind sorts.

6. **OUT OF SORTS** – These are words that have been included with the sorts but do not fit into any of the categories. They serve as an extra contrast and challenge for students who already understand word sorting.

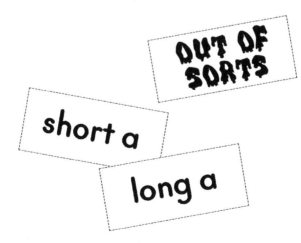

Using the Word Sorts in this Book

blackline for the students. Have them cut apart the words and sort them into the categories provided.

- Provide envelopes or plastic baggies for the students to either store the word cards or take them home to re-sort as a follow-up home-work assignment.

- Another technique for sorting with the class is to make a transparency of the sort. Have the students copy the words onto the blank word sort blackline, (pages 166-167) and then cut them apart and sort them. Or you can have them copy the words from the overhead onto lined paper they have folded into columns, or into a word study notebook.

- Students may work with partners to sort the word cards into the appropriate categories. They may then write them on a separate piece of paper or copy them into a word study note-book for reinforcement.

- You can laminate and cut apart the word sort blacklines and store them in envelopes in a *word sort learning center*. See pages 168-169 for Center Cards. You may want to keep the Answer Keys (pages 170-189) in a file in the learning center so students can either check their completed word sorts themselves or have a "designated checker" do it for them.

- Once students have completed a word sort, you can have them "hunt" in texts and envi-ronmental print to find additional words that will fit into the categories. Students may then share the words they've found with the group or class and display them on a "Word Sort" bulletin board.

- The word sort format is an excellent assess-ment tool to ensure that the word sounds, pat-terns, spelling rules and concepts you have taught have indeed been learned. Use the results to quickly identify students who need additional instruction and practice with the word sort concepts before attempting the sort again.

- You may have students revisit certain word sorts on another day by having them not only re-sort the words, but also put them in alpha-betical order once they are in the correct cate-gories. This helps build sight recognition of the words as well as practicing alphabetization skills.

- Your students can play a simple game using the word sort cards along with one die or number cube and an open-ended game board. Stack the word cards facedown. Have the stu-dents take turns picking a card and naming the category aloud. If the player chooses the cor-rect category, s/he rolls the die, and moves that number of spaces. The player who reach-es the end of the game board first is the win-ner.

| b____ | ____b |

- -

bed	bus
bat	web
rob	rib
tub	lab
bag	box
cab	but
sob	cub
bet	bell
bin	sub
rub	bee

| f____ | ____f |

- -

fit	loaf
roof	for
fed	huff
fun	fox
elf	off
fog	beef
if	fix
leaf	fat
fan	fin
wolf	puff

d____	____d

---

dot	pad
red	day
dog	dug
dim	nod
mud	dip
dig	mad
rod	dam
sad	wed
rid	do
den	kid

| c____ | h____ |

- -

he	hat
help	cot
cab	cub
cut	hop
can	had
her	hill
cop	cap
how	has
him	cat
cup	has

| g___ | ___g |

- -

girl	got
gas	gum
go	hog
bag	big
good	get
tag	pig
frog	dig
gun	gap
rug	hug
leg	dog

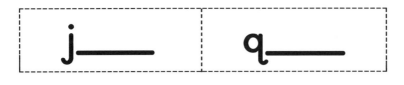

joy	quack
quilt	jet
jig	quake
just	quick
quiet	jug
quiz	queen
jump	quart
quit	jam
jog	jar
job	quail

kid	kiss
kit	took
back	kite
sink	week
look	kind
king	rock
duck	book
key	kept
lock	sack
cook	pink

leg	cool
bell	lit
lid	hill
seal	doll
owl	led
lot	feel
log	lad
tell	pool
let	lap
fill	pill

m_____   _____m

map	mop
gum	ham
mud	met
rim	dim
men	man
him	dam
mug	hem
jam	mix
mad	hum
my	mat

can	run
net	no
nag	not
fin	in
now	men
nut	win
man	ran
ten	fun
hen	pin
nip	nap

pig	cap
pin	top
cup	hop
map	pan
lap	pit
tap	nap
pat	pad
pen	up
pot	pal
zip	pet

r____	____r

- -

rod	rot
her	deer
rag	red
rat	run
jar	four
rib	our
car	door
for	rip
rig	rag
bear	star

s_____	_____s

gas	toss
sad	sit
six	this
us	sum
sub	sag
yes	sap
miss	set
boss	pass
bus	son
sat	kiss

v____	w____

- -

van	vest
we	wig
wet	wax
vase	vine
was	were
vat	wag
won	web
wing	vent
very	vote
went	win

| y___ | z___ |

yes	yam
zero	zing
zag	you
yard	year
zip	zap
yet	yank
zoo	zoom
your	yarn
yip	zone
zebra	zest

short a	short e

---

that	mad	ant
fan	tag	pet
set	am	pat
wet	leg	ten
can	led	web
went	met	sad
cat	man	bad
then	gas	rag
red	left	bed
fed	cab	van

short a	short i

as	fix	fast
mad	hid	jam
dig	had	sit
chin	has	ran
bath	hit	his
milk	map	gift
lap	rid	cap
man	fish	dad
lid	six	pink
fin	did	clap

short a	short o

back	tap	job
box	rob	hot
pop	top	ham
pat	wag	lap
glad	hat	tag
pot	fat	hop
mop	lot	dog
ran	man	sat
mom	pal	cap
not	got	fan

| t___ | ___t |

- -

top	hit
to	let
cut	jet
get	tub
bat	lot
tug	tag
tip	ten
cat	met
tan	tell
tin	but

short a	short u

- -

at	can	run
ant	sun	sung
bag	such	sad
fast	mud	mat
bug	man	ask
nut	pup	fun
but	cut	bus
sack	has	tag
sunk	van	gum
up	pal	rug

short i	short e

---

did	mix	fit
kit	bet	bed
leg	bit	him
jet	pen	set
win	pin	met
get	if	his
den	lip	ten
pig	web	pit
men	net	fed
hem	fix	sip

short i	short u

- -

hid	up	fit
big	sip	dig
bug	tin	but
cub	rich	his
fill	shut	win
sick	it	hip
run	hut	rug
drum	cup	him
us	dim	slug
must	six	tug

short i	short o

- -

pig	rob	not
pot	tin	jog
rid	fox	nod
him	mop	lid
if	lot	top
pop	rot	dot
mom	fist	rib
frog	lit	log
this	pit	six
shot	wig	dig

short o	short e

- -

den	box	lot
led	went	pond
hop	send	stop
help	let	sob
pen	not	rot
pot	rob	sent
mom	drop	hen
net	best	red
job	yes	mob
mop	ten	got

short u	short e

- -

fed	run	met
cub	sun	beg
cup	when	yes
then	jet	up
yet	hug	gum
men	nut	mud
dug	shut	elf
fun	set	ten
leg	red	bed
tub	cut	pup

short o	short u

- -

pop	tub	pot
dot	mom	chop
run	sob	pup
rug	rot	cup
us	mud	rob
up	sun	hot
not	shop	fun
top	must	tug
fox	much	stop
mug	shut	gum

short a	short i
short e	**OUT OF SORTS**

- -

sit	him	let
pink	den	jam
red	look	pit
cat	sand	win
coat	pig	set
rip	ship	map
wag	led	men
rest	leg	held
ran	sad	snap
with	lip	tan

short a	short e	short i
short o	**OUT OF SORTS**	

raft	rid	six
sob	drop	sag
test	stem	pup
son	win	van
sent	lift	cot
rich	lamp	job
run	hot	help
sad	yet	them
met	man	lost
top	bet	kept

short a	short e	**OUT OF SORTS**
short i	short o	short u

---

hut	pond	dish
raft	wish	bath
went	chin	dust
yes	pest	gum
just	milk	dip
test	mom	get
sand	lost	bus
see	rich	look
soft	swam	top
cap	plum	belt

short a	short e	**OUT OF SORTS**
short i	short o	short u

wet	rush	felt
slid	fix	took
bed	clock	gift
dock	grab	stop
went	like	bump
frog	fist	camp
twig	drop	bath
seat	glad	brag
thud	best	cute
shut	fish	gum

short a	short e	**OUT OF SORTS**
short i	short o	short u

cap	hunt	row
fed	cars	sun
shut	box	them
clock	his	hand
hot	pan	sent
rip	left	right
good	next	ask
will	not	down
job	inch	best
run	did	swam

short a	short e	OUT OF SORTS
short i	short o	short u

---

jump	fox	trip
him	fun	lot
sink	like	hunt
got	crab	sand
could	dress	bird
sick	get	sock
up	boy	fill
hat	can	hut
help	farm	mat
hop	well	leg

short a	short e	OUT OF SORTS

ran	stand	went
glad	sit	cut
look	nest	end
bent	held	plan
spent	dash	ask
neck	past	sat
sand	self	no
lap	help	camp
met	my	can
yell	left	fell

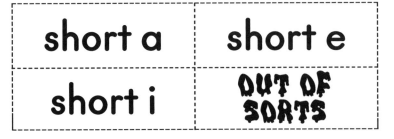

short a	short e
short i	**OUT OF SORTS**

- -

sled	risk	help
self	spin	spend
glad	dish	act
these	fed	cry
track	him	sent
stick	sad	less
crib	that	itch
still	step	man
great	day	book
sink	bend	damp

short a	short e	short i
short o	**OUT OF SORTS**	

- -

box	clock	map
rod	rock	nest
will	slid	bell
kiss	chill	by
fog	boat	toy
bath	his	foot
wax	grin	step
sled	lot	had
bad	stem	snack
them	lend	choose

short a	short e	OUT OF SORTS
short i	short o	short u

stop	rent	track
slid	soft	scab
red	back	stem
sky	cliff	led
hip	will	burn
dump	cute	rung
dot	drink	nose
help	rod	mud
camp	fox	truck
clap	these	spun

short a	short e	**OUT OF SORTS**
short i	short o	short u

crash	scuff	wish
skunk	jump	hot
stop	club	end
smell	blend	boy
check	hand	say
hug	lit	goose
black	ship	me
mad	dish	elf
spent	mash	could
skip	shop	class

short a	short e	**OUT OF SORTS**
short i	short o	short u

plum	pie	say
club	milk	tan
rock	well	wag
block	bug	fish
black	us	six
mend	sheep	you
leg	box	cut
fill	band	no
egg	snap	lock
will	lamp	trot

short a	long a

- -

cake	track	swam
cat	rake	trap
can	ask	shake
take	glad	camp
than	made	plane
lane	quack	tale
age	mad	whale
bath	flag	pale
stand	grape	plant
same	last	shade

short a	long a

pat	fat	sad
shade	ham	made
plate	lake	rag
can	cab	has
sale	back	had
hand	name	game
gate	sand	rack
make	snake	man
bag	map	bake
cane	take	late

short e	long e

- -

get	men	tree
seem	queen	meat
step	let	year
tell	fed	seal
beak	left	neck
deep	bed	sweet
week	tent	real
leg	green	beg
each	held	red
feel	feet	east

short e	long e

- -

led	went	heat
left	jeep	hear
meet	bead	hen
men	clean	deck
weak	jet	steal
mean	them	dear
send	kept	sled
seed	bend	need
wet	help	leave
team	wheel	held

short i	long i

- -

sip	time	night
life	pin	fire
lift	him	rib
dig	sink	big
hide	mile	sky
did	wise	gift
tight	hit	ride
sick	kiss	kid
fine	chin	cry
like	nine	dime

short i	long i

- -

hike	win	mind
nine	five	fin
hit	swim	fine
tin	time	rise
miss	my	lick
tire	kick	dish
like	nice	right
ship	pig	fire
pine	hill	ripe
pink	hint	find

short o	long o

- -

top	hop	toe
rope	roll	hole
frog	lost	home
soak	moth	knock
toad	nose	job
go	note	coat
boat	box	gold
dog	not	rose
nod	hope	drop
cold	woke	cross

short o	long o

boss	pond	fox
note	broke	spot
crop	stole	stop
got	mop	bone
rode	toast	clock
nod	wore	rob
no	lost	smoke
croak	cloth	boat
mole	rose	pole
hog	dove	go

short u	long u

- -

tub	tube	fuse
gruff	mule	dude
rude	shut	cube
mud	tune	much
gum	hunt	duck
jump	June	hut
sung	glue	blue
lunch	but	rule
rug	duke	pup
use	bump	fun

short u	long u

- -

junk	fluke	tube
use	bug	thud
June	brush	cub
trunk	skull	plum
hunt	cup	run
rule	flute	glue
skunk	fuse	mug
cut	bus	dump
cute	blue	must
tune	huff	mule

short a	long a	long e

grab	beat	wag
blade	stamp	clash
bake	pail	train
wade	way	skate
these	sweep	teach
seem	flat	damp
plan	band	sleep
feed	leaf	say
leave	squeak	date
branch	me	snake

short a	short e	
long a	long e	long o

cab	sell	steep
came	meat	coat
sack	bed	pack
neck	hat	best
gate	broke	pets
rope	bone	send
save	tape	leaf
trap	these	stone
beet	sleep	rain
late	road	map

short a	short e	short i	
long a	long e	long i	long o

man	ride	shade
ten	big	whale
him	best	white
plane	men	these
same	hope	Pete
pole	six	stone
smoke	maps	five
chase	did	broke
pipe	ripe	sleep
meal	leaf	that

short a	short e	long a	long e
short i	short o	long i	long o
			long u

pet	sale	use
bed	game	bike
stop	bride	hat
kite	rip	mule
wave	mad	bit
cube	hole	feel
cute	these	home
not	seal	broke
when	twin	meal
top	pal	stage

short a	short e	long a	long e
short i	short o	long i	long o
	short u	long u	

rob	cub	plate
tap	cube	grape
hen	fin	clean
fine	snake	bus
code	stroke	toast
slice	mule	wrap
these	cheap	stick
this	wheel	home
that	cut	pot
smile	pet	fun

short a	short e	long a	long e
short i	short o	long i	long o
	short u	long u	

pop	white	goal
jug	bent	moan
mom	flame	wipe
pen	date	mope
rat	free	drive
rate	clean	cute
pup	bead	splash
sob	brain	swim
set	glad	mule
hit	thin	toad

short a	short e
long a	long e

cash	green	me
catch	send	fast
best	help	street
jail	snack	came
feels	than	plain
date	these	need
real	sand	made
teeth	seed	rain
sleep	face	fresh
wrap	meat	yet

short a	short e	short i	short o
long a	long e	long i	long o

- -

fan	mix	kiss
led	five	loss
that	green	stick
fine	nine	week
past	stage	wade
slice	knock	rose
lamb	broke	note
hens	clock	not
rent	sail	win
clean	snake	cone

short a	short e	long a	long e
short i	short o	long i	long o
short u			

crop	cheek	time
trip	pick	these
train	stung	wife
rob	with	date
robe	slope	same
fond	nest	grape
brat	grand	bride
west	run	meet
stack	home	miss
check	fade	road

short a	short e	long a	long e
short i	short o	long i	long o
short u		long u	**OUT OF SORTS**

seem	cute	crib
wait	Fred	melt
street	glad	stuff
toad	spot	threw
side	next	rung
proud	frog	nuts
drive	these	main
cape	this	cube
hat	those	June
spoke	swim	hand

long a	long e	long u
long i	long o	**OUT OF SORTS**

train	fire	pipe
beat	make	stone
creep	pill	ask
queen	raise	snail
chose	deep	cube
ride	gave	use
nice	must	clock
poke	jeep	mule
help	cone	fuse
drove	slide	cute

ack	ank	ap	an
	ash	at	OUT OF SORTS

shack	play	wrap
pack	tack	snack
can	man	plan
map	make	crash
cash	that	chat
name	saw	flat
back	trash	slap
bank	tank	ran
rash	snap	thank
cap	flash	brat

long a	long e	long i
long o	long u	**OUT OF SORTS**

woke	rose	came
stove	nine	paint
that	green	pie
side	beach	use
mule	plate	fog
wait	dime	cute
cheap	sleep	cube
these	hope	pat
cut	stone	set
may	wise	brave

an	ap
ack	ank

back	track	thank
can	map	drank
nap	tan	stack
sank	black	lap
snap	pan	clap
man	than	shack
fan	snack	rank
ran	trap	tank
bank	crack	quack
rap	plan	pack

ash	at
and	all

---

cash	mat	stall
call	tall	mash
ball	dash	flat
crash	trash	band
hand	pat	stand
cat	that	squall
fall	smash	grand
small	flash	slash
land	brat	brand
hat	wall	strand

ack	ank	an	ap
	at	ash	**OUT OF SORTS**

lap	sank	tack
rash	chat	dash
bank	crash	scan
cat	say	tap
flat	rat	plan
that	cane	trash
cake	mash	snap
span	thank	smash
back	than	with
shack	map	late

est	ell	en
et	ent	end

ten	spend	shell
send	men	get
spent	test	nest
bend	bent	pet
when	tent	cent
west	yell	fell
sent	then	let
set	mend	smell
hen	rest	blend
bell	lent	guest

est	ell	en	et
	ent	end	**OUT OF SORTS**

let	nest	well
tell	nice	chest
bent	lend	set
hen	dent	do
best	when	tent
sent	spell	spend
sell	see	bet
test	rest	ten
shell	get	itch
pen	men	mend

ick	ill	in	ing
	ink	ip	it

kick	thin	skin
win	pick	chill
tip	fill	hip
sit	wing	stick
pit	pink	spring
sip	chin	drink
sink	spill	ship
pin	swing	lit
pill	thing	bit
still	think	thick

ick	ill	in	ing
ink	ip	it	**OUT OF SORTS**

sick	trip	knit
pink	thick	blink
pot	fit	skip
sip	make	swing
wink	chin	spill
string	thin	kite
think	will	chill
thing	stick	quit
twin	hit	so
quick	king	spin

ock	op
ot	og

hot	got	chop
fog	not	shock
rock	shop	jog
dog	dock	crop
hog	drop	dot
pot	spot	knock
sock	block	smog
log	frog	trot
clock	knot	flop
stop	mop	stock

ock	op	ot
	og	**OUT OF SORTS**

rock	frog	pop
spot	stock	lock
dog	stop	mop
fog	dock	chop
hop	knock	smog
clock	jog	got
told	shop	knot
log	shot	use
lot	ice	dot
make	block	shock

uck	ug
ump	unk

duck	sunk	mug
bump	truck	struck
junk	pump	drug
skunk	stump	slug
jump	hug	plump
bunk	dunk	thump
lug	stuck	plug
luck	cluck	hunk
lump	chunk	shrug
snug	trunk	slump

uck	ug	ump
	unk	**OUT OF SORTS**

sunk	dump	plug
tuck	truck	snug
go	bug	lump
cluck	duck	chunk
trunk	mug	slump
bump	pump	junk
the	plump	luck
bunk	may	at
slug	dunk	skunk
stuck	drug	stump

ank	ink	unk

---

bank	prank	skunk
sunk	tank	clink
stink	rank	link
spank	blink	crank
pink	drunk	thank
trunk	junk	hunk
wink	think	punk
bunk	chunk	drank
plank	mink	dunk
sank	sink	rink

bl	pl	sl	fl
	gl	cl	**OUT OF SORTS**

---

slab	plum	club
clump	clam	late
clip	glad	blink
went	slept	glob
floor	glum	flesh
block	slam	cut
slap	its	plant
flat	Glenn	plan
fling	plug	blend
sled	blank	flip

br	gr	cr	dr
fr	tr	pr	**OUT OF SORTS**

prop	print	trap
drag	grin	trunk
drum	from	crust
clock	trot	front
crush	trip	jump
green	grip	brim
grass	crib	brag
bring	brat	pop
frog	drift	free
crash	drank	prom

bl	cl	fl	
br	cr	fr	**OUT OF SORTS**

---

blast	brat	blank
free	crib	flat
clip	frog	flag
crab	friend	crop
flip	cloth	bent
brag	blink	from
was	brim	frost
bring	brush	crash
blend	can	flush
clam	clap	read

gl	pl	sl	OUT OF SORTS
gr	pr	dr	tr

glad	drum	prop
grand	slept	house
sled	book	gland
plan	slid	trunk
proud	print	prod
cat	drop	grunt
drag	slot	trust
grin	glob	plum
trap	trim	plug
glass	drip	glum

sc	st	sk	sm
sn	sp	sw	**OUT OF SORTS**

---

scab	stem	stunt
swift	skid	scar
skin	skate	scalp
small	some	swim
snap	snip	hats
swing	spot	spank
stand	spent	stop
smog	skip	cup
sweet	snug	scan
smell	spin	lake

sc	sk	sm
	sn	**OUT OF SORTS**

skim	smell	skit
sure	snip	smug
smog	sit	smile
snail	smash	snug
snag	skin	smoke
skip	skid	snake
snap	scalp	sat
skunk	seat	scales
small	scab	skill
scan	some	skirt

sn	st	sw
	sp	**OUT OF SORTS**

----

swam	sting	swamp
still	swell	swift
stock	snore	snip
snake	speak	stir
step	spy	snag
sent	same	spin
steep	sweep	spent
spill	spark	sing
sneak	snap	sale
stack	swap	sunk

ch	sh	OUT OF SORTS

- -

shark	child	chair
chart	chat	shy
cut	cheese	shoe
shine	ship	sheep
shin	cat	chew
chip	chin	chest
shoot	chop	sail
sit	shell	shed
shut	sharp	cheap
shout	check	cherry

wh	th	**OUT OF SORTS**

- -

when	which	while
what	thank	white
then	where	than
that	they	this
was	their	tent
think	those	wheat
thin	went	whack
these	them	why
wheel	the	whip
whale	toe	whistle

ch	sh
th	wh

- -

what	chin	chimp
chick	chat	shell
shut	short	than
them	shot	which
they	that	thump
when	this	should
whip	chunk	chest
shop	shed	those
shelf	chop	while
why	thing	wheel

ch	sh
th	wh

- -

chill	why	while
ship	that	sheep
shell	this	shut
what	check	thorn
when	she	cherry
thin	chose	chunk
thing	thick	whale
chat	shark	wheat
short	where	thank
cheap	should	child

ch	sh	th
	wh	OUT OF SORTS

---

shade	chest	white
when	shout	shark
wham	tub	wheel
than	this	whale
that	chop	whine
cats	shop	child
chomp	thick	was
shut	cheat	cheer
what	short	thumb
chew	third	sits

____ch	____sh	____th

with	math	inch
beach	cash	leash
much	moth	each
wash	lunch	north
ranch	teach	worth
rush	tooth	itch
path	trash	bush
wish	dish	booth
sixth	south	such
push	bench	brush

| sh____ | ch____ | th____ |
| ____sh | ____ch | ____th |

much	chick	chain
chest	tooth	smash
that	push	such
bath	shy	cheap
crash	shack	dish
wash	thumb	think
shell	with	path
shout	bush	sixth
chin	thorn	share
itch	thick	both

s	es

- -

cats	pens	lashes
girls	catches	pets
cups	wigs	mashes
wishes	dresses	pigs
boys	sons	witches
latches	mats	passes
paths	itches	pups
fishes	cuts	matches
nets	shells	glasses
pins	patches	brushes

s	es	ing

- -

glasses	looking	clocks
jumping	chips	selling
passes	seeing	witches
dresses	reads	filling
dogs	sleeping	marching
frogs	beeps	hatches
boots	weeks	farming
ducks	rocking	dishes
fishes	socks	dashes
messes	ticking	fishing

ing	ed	**OUT OF SORTS**

- -

jumping	pinching	leaking
going	sees	wanted
singing	acted	peeling
seeing	forming	slowed
dress	thanked	cheering
reading	painted	thinking
rowed	walking	first
coloring	covered	spelled
chewed	laughing	backed
guessed	greeted	rained

| ed | doubled final consonant + ed |
| ing | doubled final consonant + ing |

running	wished	batting
raked	cutting	flagged
going	ringing	spinning
chopped	dotted	nesting
stopped	patting	drifted
talking	batted	helped
packed	melting	padded
cooling	spending	lapping
waited	skipped	jammed
flopping	crashing	dragging

singular nouns
plural nouns

hat	kisses	gift
bugs	shark	jars
ropes	plates	lunches
frog	turtles	rocks
dogs	boxes	pools
hole	bushes	cow
dots	net	wagon
letter	waves	star
birds	planes	lid
desk	tent	tack

singular nouns
plural nouns

- -

tooth	mouse	moose
sheep	teeth	men
seals	feet	woman
lion	radios	man
clowns	babies	hour
lemon	fishes	goose
mice	bus	baby
toys	child	moose
geese	deer	story
children	sheep	deer

contractions
not contractions

can't	she's	could
is	isn't	not
hasn't	we'll	they
cannot	they're	aren't
it's	didn't	hadn't
are	should	haven't
let's	won't	has
I've	don't	did
may	we've	what
I'm	doesn't	have

compound
not compound

- -

cannot	inside	indoor
into	cookbook	football
painting	someone	suntan
jellyfish	them	playing
daytime	tugboat	today
boy	bike	bedroom
airport	seashell	doorbell
myself	skipping	looked
girls	sees	key
jumping	snowball	teeth

compound
not compound

cannot	backyard	pillow
cowboy	horse	dresses
sailboat	sunny	seagull
chairs	mother	farmer
hilltop	outfit	house
snowman	wind	trees
without	anyone	brushes
boxes	goldfish	water
bullfrog	butterfly	lakes
cupcake	somehow	tables

contractions
compound words

- -

can't	I've	doesn't
isn't	what's	hadn't
inside	snowman	everyone
I'll	seashell	itself
baseball	indoor	without
she'll	wheelchair	wouldn't
we'll	they've	won't
didn't	herself	you've
into	homesick	flashlight
cannot	it's	sunshine

contractions	**OUT OF SORTS**

compound words

- -

don't	can't	nobody
anyone	doesn't	dugout
seesaw	into	hilltop
runs	daytime	you've
tryout	there's	who's
isn't	hadn't	homemade
seeing	let's	teammate
sunrise	softball	wrote
outside	what's	sit
crosswalk	haven't	I'll

ail	ain
ake	ale

bail	pail	chain
main	stake	rail
take	whale	stain
cake	fake	brake
male	pain	bale
lake	hail	strain
fail	rain	snail
brain	quake	pale
jail	snake	scale
tale	sale	trail

ame	ate	ay

fame	stay	tray
gate	rate	flame
hay	tame	crate
may	state	stray
date	gray	late
pray	spray	frame
name	plate	blame
fate	slay	lame
same	skate	game
hate	jay	came

ail	ain	ake	ale
ame	ate	ay	

pail	flame	quake
shake	snake	tale
main	skate	shame
name	gray	scale
game	whale	stray
plate	blame	stale
stay	flake	frail
stain	crate	quail
chain	trail	spray
snail	plain	Spain

ail	ain	ake	ale
ame	ate	ay	

shame	sake	sprain
shake	jail	frame
scale	brain	whale
late	stale	sail
sale	flake	skate
stain	lame	nail
blame	crate	tame
stay	pray	plate
mail	frail	gate
plain	gray	sway

eat	eek	eed
eep	een	

---

queen	neat	Greek
peek	treat	seen
wheat	steep	weed
seed	need	screen
feed	speed	teen
green	sweep	sleep
weep	beat	heat
cheek	deep	sheen
week	creek	reek
bleed	beep	cleat

eel	eeze	ear
eak	eet	

feet	squeeze	wheeze
beak	leak	speak
feel	peel	sneak
breeze	dear	wheel
beet	greet	clear
sleet	freeze	tweeze
peak	fear	smear
kneel	steel	heel
sneeze	hear	creak
meet	spear	sheet

east	eal	ead	eap
	ee	eave	eech

see	lead	deal
beast	knee	steal
leap	leech	knead
heal	fee	squeal
speech	heap	leave
bee	plead	weave
cheap	meal	screech
heave	flee	yeast
real	bead	reap
feast	read	least

ice	ide
ight	ine

light	fright	shine
nice	mice	bride
pride	side	glide
fine	slight	mine
slide	ride	dice
slice	spice	price
flight	bright	whine
line	tide	knight
right	spine	twice
nine	swine	stride

ile	ime	ipe
ite	ive	ike

- -

mile	Mike	wipe
like	lime	swipe
ripe	gripe	while
five	spike	slime
pile	white	strike
dive	strive	pike
chime	quite	vile
write	stripe	mime
drive	crime	bite
grime	file	thrive

ide	ime	ine
ipe	ive	ike

hive	crime	spine
time	stripe	strive
like	vine	drive
hide	lime	strike
wipe	tide	shine
chime	dive	dime
swipe	bride	slide
glide	pine	whine
slime	pride	ripe
nine	bike	thrive

oke	ore	oat
ode	old	one

cone	cold	spoke
goat	bone	stroke
gold	code	snore
core	stone	throat
smoke	hold	scold
rode	more	boat
coat	chore	strode
store	phone	pore
broke	told	yoke
float	choke	mode

ope	ow	ote
ove	ome	ose

home	clove	gnome
those	chose	snow
wove	low	stove
hope	mope	grove
rope	dome	crow
wrote	cove	close
Rome	blow	chrome
scope	note	cope
vote	slope	nose
know	slow	pose

ose	ope	one
	oat	oke

nose	bloat	shone
hope	chose	zone
smoke	rope	scope
rose	joke	spoke
cone	bone	hose
coke	mope	poke
cope	boat	lone
slope	choke	phone
goat	float	prose
moat	pose	throat

ue	ule	ume	une
	use	ute	ube

cute	brute	lute
tune	flute	clue
blue	yule	flue
mute	fume	June
prune	hue	use
fuse	sue	cube
due	plume	rule
abuse	chute	tube
glue	jute	spume
muse	true	mule

er	ir	ur

- -

germ	church	nurse
bird	jerk	verse
term	skirt	first
dirt	turn	purse
fern	firm	surf
hurt	nerve	clerk
flirt	stir	curve
curl	shirt	stern
fir	curb	thirst
spurt	perch	swerve

ar	or

---

dark	worn	carve
march	harp	horse
born	part	forth
chart	porch	shark
cart	card	torch
north	pork	start
port	fort	cord
park	harm	cork
large	storm	barge
short	charm	sport

ar	or

- -

born	far	sharp
north	lord	dark
farm	card	more
form	sore	torn
park	shore	ore
fork	for	barn
horn	short	bark
tar	cart	march
corn	arm	yard
port	mark	yarn

ar	er	ir
ur	or	

- -

shark	nurse	birth
skirt	sport	large
horse	march	north
lark	nerve	burst
fern	serve	thorn
force	blurt	harm
firm	carve	chirp
blur	perk	term
turn	bird	swirl
cord	curve	verse

ar	er	ir
ur	or	**OUT OF SORTS**

firm	curl	storm
perch	born	snarl
burn	verse	term
mark	harm	party
here	fern	quirk
sharp	scarf	fire
blur	churn	gorge
squirt	shirt	nurse
clerk	stern	third
barb	bear	porch

ai	ay	ei

frail	eight	neigh
sway	tray	paint
veil	grain	strait
gray	sleigh	vein
weight	clay	may
rein	waist	maid
play	spray	freight
trail	slay	ray
stray	plain	quaint
bait	faith	eighth

ai	ay
ei	OUT OF SORTS

---

snail	pet	saint
stray	sway	sleigh
weight	praise	gray
waist	vein	rein
want	play	chose
quaint	veil	clay
way	paint	neigh
tray	weigh	mat
sprain	eight	freight
straight	pay	trail

ee	ea
e	ie

---

seal	grief	we
he	wheat	shriek
field	week	weep
beef	beach	kneel
leash	peace	piece
flea	green	thief
seem	three	squeak
she	shield	street
niece	stream	me
weave	cheese	be

ee	ea	ie
	e	OUT OF SORTS

tea	men	sleeve
yield	feast	teach
me	greet	speech
siege	least	field
set	stream	shriek
weed	went	sleet
speak	thief	he
wheel	sneak	piece
leak	she	we
queen	teeth	fed

igh	___y
i **with 2 consonants**	

high	night	knight
my	spy	rind
climb	find	bind
wild	sigh	thigh
sly	fly	light
right	sign	blind
cry	sight	bright
child	try	sky
fry	dry	grind
fight	kind	spry

igh	____y	**OUT OF SORTS**
i with 2 consonants		

- -

shy	pry	thigh
sign	fly	wild
hid	tight	cry
my	find	may
grind	child	spy
why	mild	night
slight	its	spry
climb	try	flight
bright	might	kind
high	sky	sit

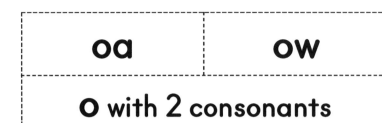

oa	ow
o with 2 consonants	

road	soak	roach
sold	poll	stroll
both	know	groan
loaf	coal	own
toad	cold	grow
post	coat	comb
roll	shown	flown
loan	known	bowl
host	moat	growth
jolt	ghost	bolt

oa	ow	OUT OF SORTS
o with 2 consonants		

goat	soak	own
mob	roll	log
oath	growth	blown
ghost	cot	fold
soap	post	mop
know	both	snow
road	loan	hold
flown	folk	croak
load	show	host
throw	roast	thrown

ue	ui	u_e

---

blue	flue	glue
dude	bruise	rude
cue	hue	June
rule	duke	plume
suit	crude	rue
due	true	fume
tube	cruise	tune
fruit	clue	truce
spruce	brute	chute
prune	sue	juice

ue	ui
u_e	OUT OF SORTS

suit	duke	fume
tune	flue	hue
June	cue	clue
due	plume	dune
pup	glue	yule
tube	juice	put
bruise	fruit	burn
dude	blue	jump
cruise	rule	flute
sue	crude	full

ea	ew

bread	tread	spread
dew	threw	deaf
dead	wealth	drew
few	lead	blew
sweat	feather	screw
thread	new	meant
stew	flew	death
crew	stealth	heather
brew	dread	shrewd
breath	shrew	knew

oo (*moo*)	oo (*book*)

bloom	fool	good
zoo	wool	smooth
coop	proof	zoom
room	spoon	look
hoot	stood	brook
crook	cook	hoof
took	school	troop
noon	shook	roost
scoot	mood	hood
wood	moon	goof

oy	oi

- -

toy	void	soy
coin	joint	boil
spoil	toil	joist
joy	coy	coil
oil	hoist	toys
foil	join	boys
point	ploy	joys
Roy	soil	points
boy	broil	coins
moist	groin	boils

glow	town	blow
plow	down	howl
low	how	scowl
show	stow	owl
brown	snow	tow
know	growl	crown
row	wow	brow
clown	grow	flow
slow	crow	prowl
fowl	mow	known

ou	ow

found	plow	south
bound	scowl	doubt
wow	mound	how
brown	cloud	pouch
cow	clown	scout
proud	growl	drown
down	town	vow
owl	loud	ground
sprout	sound	round
count	now	grouch

au	aw

haul	straw	lawn
paw	squawk	saw
gauze	haunt	jaunt
drawn	vault	launch
claw	jaw	cause
hawk	thaw	shawl
raw	gnaw	draw
taught	fault	gaudy
fraud	caught	haunch
crawl	dawn	pause

au	aw	al

---

yawn	chalk	paw
caught	taught	gauze
talk	false	haunt
haul	gnaw	fraud
hawk	malt	scald
halt	crawl	hall
lawn	fault	draw
launch	salt	waltz
saw	stalk	vault
walk	small	sprawl

scr	shr	spl	spr
	squ	str	thr

scrunch	split	thrust
shrank	strap	splotch
squirt	sprain	shrimp
straight	squeal	scroll
shriek	throat	shrill
stream	squid	squad
thread	squint	splash
throw	stress	script
shrug	splurge	sprang
screen	sprint	spring

scr	shr	spl	spr
squ	str	thr	

stripe	script	stray
shroud	thrive	thrill
throne	splurge	squeal
squirt	strike	squint
scrimp	split	thrush
sprang	shred	sprout
stride	scroll	squid
threat	scram	splint
shrunk	shrank	scribe
spread	stream	splash

| ___ck | ___ke | ___k |

---

beak	tack	milk
track	wink	sneak
dock	kick	crack
flake	make	desk
week	choke	thick
check	skunk	pork
take	quake	sleek
stick	quack	truck
fake	park	like
woke	lake	spoke

Sound-Alike Endings: ck, ke, k

___ck	___ke	___k

---

shake	stuck	sick
knock	wake	block
bark	junk	stalk
shook	click	spoke
make	hike	bike
deck	sleek	milk
leak	quick	stick
pork	book	brick
pack	joke	smoke
rake	stalk	flake

____ck	____ke	____k

spark	weak	smoke
week	deck	strike
black	spoke	lick
bake	dark	hike
track	struck	stuck
neck	fake	fork
sank	like	slack
poke	cheek	luck
sneak	croak	flake
smack	broke	wreck

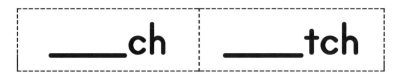

_____ch | _____tch

- -

lunch	batch	switch
latch	match	gulch
bench	march	crutch
peach	scratch	torch
patch	ditch	fetch
branch	reach	witch
catch	church	munch
pitch	stitch	watch
crunch	pouch	punch
teach	sketch	clutch

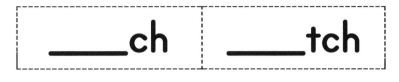

scorch	bench	snatch
switch	fetch	pinch
beach	teach	reach
catch	scratch	ditch
batch	lunch	drench
crunch	witch	stitch
hitch	porch	hitch
watch	branch	blotch
munch	sketch	latch
search	hunch	church

_____ge   _____dge

trudge	edge	stooge
range	change	huge
large	page	fudge
sage	pledge	cage
badge	ridge	hinge
stage	charge	budge
bridge	rage	dodge
judge	nudge	gouge
plunge	wedge	hedge
ledge	lodge	fringe

gn____	kn____
wr____	____mb

gnash	lamb	knead
limb	write	dumb
wrap	wreath	knot
knob	kneel	gnarl
gnat	crumb	wrist
wrote	gnaw	wreck
comb	knee	wrong
tomb	gnu	knelt
knack	thumb	wring
gnome	knight	bomb

ed *(dated)*	d *(tried)*	t *(mixed)*

walked	planted	rented
joined	fished	sailed
roasted	combed	stamped
passed	melted	worked
needed	bumped	boiled
rained	squirted	lasted
snowed	grabbed	started
picked	rolled	cleaned
asked	crushed	smiled
rushed	splashed	twisted

ed (*dated*)	d (*tried*)	t (*mixed*)

---

acted	skipped	mixed
asked	coached	pushed
aimed	parted	baked
winked	mailed	splashed
batted	fished	seemed
wilted	crushed	trusted
yelled	trailed	rolled
picked	treated	crowed
shifted	melted	waited
showed	missed	groaned

number words	color words

red	one	thirteen
blue	twelve	four
purple	black	gray
ten	brown	tan
pink	white	seven
nine	eight	seventy
three	eleven	navy
six	orange	teal
yellow	five	ninety
green	violet	thousand

farm animals	zoo animals

tiger	lamb	gorilla
cow	puppy	pony
horse	piglet	crocodile
elephant	dog	python
sheep	rooster	alligator
giraffe	cat	calf
pig	zebra	hippo
lion	kitten	panda
hyena	chick	bear
chicken	monkey	koala

land vehicles	air vehicles

water vehicles

balloon	submarine	skateboard
truck	sailboat	canoe
jet	train	bus
jet ski	ship	surfboard
airplane	helicopter	ferryboat
car	tricycle	tugboat
cab	bike	motorcycle
roller skates	wagon	biplane
tractor	trailer	water skis
blimp	rocket	rowboat

has wheels
does not have wheels

bike	book	cab
table	truck	shoes
car	tractor	pots
roller skates	pen	tricycle
glass	flower	skateboard
wagon	cup	horse
plane	train	bus
plate	pig	jar
jet	jeep	dog
paper	taxi	cow

days of the week	time words
months of the year	

- -

June	February	Friday
Thursday	morning	Saturday
today	Sunday	July
October	tomorrow	August
May	November	calendar
Tuesday	week	year
December	January	dates
months	yesterday	weekly
March	September	before
Wednesday	Monday	April

living things
non-living things

table	pen	fish
trees	kitten	cloud
cat	pig	room
dog	picture	puppy
flowers	ball	chair
window	cow	book
dress	bug	rabbit
door	hat	bird
glass	flag	mouse
snake	bike	parrot

animal mothers	animal babies

gosling	horse	nestling
salmon	puppy	goose
foal	owl	goat
cat	tadpole	dog
bear	kitten	eaglet
kid	piglet	cow
chick	robin	owlet
duckling	calf	cub
pig	eagle	hen
frog	duck	fingerling

city words

country words

banks	factories	skyscrapers
tractor	corn fields	crops
chickens	cows	subway
city buses	traffic	pasture
concrete	freeway	silo
sheep	haystacks	escalators
airport	trolley	malls
plow	stadium	farmer
crowds	taxi	barn
neon sign	horses	pigs

water words
land words

sea	cliff	grassland
pond	tide	prairie
lake	island	volcano
plain	shore	waves
hill	bayou	raindrop
mountain	gulf	puddle
river	continent	dunes
stream	peninsula	waterfall
ocean	desert	rapids
creek	bay	canyon

summer words
winter words

---

beach	swimming	suntan
snowfall	ice-skating	picnics
icy	mittens	snowshoes
freezing	surfing	gloves
hot	scuba	blizzard
sunny	fan	frosty
snowman	toboggan	water ski
frigid	sunburn	baseball
wind-chill	icicles	sandcastles
warm	sleet	watermelon

Appendix

Directions for a
Closed Word Sort

Materials
word sort cards
category cards or "key word" cards

Directions
1. Place the word sort category cards or the "key word" cards at the top of the table.
2. Place the word sort cards on the table.
3. Think about the categories as you look carefully at each word sort card and say the word slowly.
4. As you say the word, listen for the sound parts that are shown on the category cards.
5. Place the word sort card under the category it matches.
6. Sort all of the word cards this way.
7. If there are words that do not fit into any of the categories, place them in an "out of sorts" category.
8. Have someone check your sorts.

short a	short e	OUT OF SORTS
mad	bed	pig
pat	leg	
cat	web	

Learning Center Card

Directions for an
Open Word Sort

Materials
word sort cards
blank category cards

Directions
1. Place the word sort cards on the table.
2. Look carefully at all of the cards and say the words slowly.
3. Think about how some of the words might be alike.
4. Place those cards together and write how the words are alike on a blank category card. Place the category card above the words that fit in that category. Sort the rest of the word cards this way.
5. If there are any word sort cards that do not fit into any of the categories, make an "out of sorts" category card and place those word sort cards under it.
6. Have someone check your work.

short a	*short e*	*out of sorts*
hope	cube	cut
rose	cute	fog
stone	mule	

Answer Keys:

Consonant Sorts (#1-#16)

#1
b___	___b
bag	cab
bat	cub
bed	lab
bee	rib
bell	rob
bet	rub
bin	sob
box	sub
bus	tub
but	web

#2
d—	___d
dam	kid
day	mad
den	mud
dig	nod
dim	pad
dip	red
do	rid
dog	rod
dot	sad
dug	wed

#3
f___	___f
fan	beef
fat	elf
fed	huff
fin	if
fit	leaf
fix	loaf
fog	off
for	puff
fox	roof
fun	wolf

#4
g___	___g
gap	bag
gas	big
get	dig
girl	dog
go	frog
good	hog
got	hug
gum	leg
gun	pig
	rug
	tag

#5
c___	h___
cab	had
can	has
cap	hat
cat	he
cop	help
cot	her
cub	hill
cup	him
cut	hop
	hot
	how

#6
j___	q___
jam	quack
jar	quail
jet	quake
jig	quart
job	queen
jog	quick
joy	quiet
jug	quilt
jump	quit
just	quiz

#7
k___	___k
kept	back
key	book
kid	cook
kind	duck
king	lock
kiss	look
kit	pink
kite	rock
	sack
	sink
	took
	week

#8
l___	___l
lad	bell
lap	cool
led	doll
leg	feel
let	fill
lid	hill
lit	owl
log	pill
lot	pool
	seal
	tell

#9
m___	___m
mad	dam
man	dim
map	gum
mat	ham
men	hem
met	him
mix	hum
mop	jam
mud	rim
mug	
my	

#10
n___	___n
nag	can
nap	fin
net	fun
nip	hen
no	in
not	man
now	men
nut	pin
	ran
	run
	ten
	win

#11
p___	___p
pad	cap
pal	cup
pan	hop
pat	lap
pen	map
pet	nap
pig	tap
pin	top
pit	up
pot	zip

#12
r___	___r
rag	bear
rap	car
rat	deer
red	door
rib	for
rig	four
rip	her
rod	jar
rot	our
run	star

#13
s___	___s
sad	boss
sag	bus
sap	gas
sat	kiss
set	miss
sit	pass
six	this
son	toss
sub	us
sum	yes

#14
t___	___t
tag	bat
tan	but
tell	cat
ten	cut
tin	get
tip	hit
to	jet
top	let
tub	lot
tug	met

#15
v___	w___
van	wag
vase	was
vat	wax
vent	we
very	web
vest	went
vine	were
vote	wet
	wig
	win
	wing
	won

#16
y___	z___
yam	zag
yank	zap
yard	zebra
yarn	zero
year	zest
yes	zing
yet	zip
yip	zone
you	zoo
your	zoom

Answer Keys:

Vowel Sorts (#17–#28)

#17

short a	short e
am	bed
ant	fed
bad	led
cab	left
can	leg
cat	met
fan	pet
gas	red
mad	set
man	ten
pat	then
rag	web
sad	went
tag	wet
that	
van	

#18

short a	short i
as	chin
bath	did
cap	dig
clap	fin
dad	fish
fast	fix
had	gift
has	hid
jam	his
lap	hit
mad	lid
man	milk
map	pink
ran	rid
	sit
	six

#19

short a	short o
back	box
cap	dog
fan	got
fat	hop
glad	hot
ham	job
hat	lot
lap	mom
man	mop
pal	not
pat	pop
ran	pot
sat	rob
tag	top
tap	
wag	

#20

short a	short u
ant	bug
ask	bus
at	but
bag	cut
can	fun
fast	gum
has	mud
man	nut
mat	pup
pal	rug
sack	run
sad	such
tag	sun
van	sung
	sunk
	up

#21

short i	short e
bit	bed
did	bet
fit	den
fix	fed
him	get
his	hem
if	jet
kit	leg
lip	men
mix	met
pig	net
pin	pen
pit	set
sip	ten
win	web

#22

short i	short o
dig	pot
fist	dot
him	fox
if	frog
lid	jog
lit	log
pig	lot
pit	mom
rib	mop
rid	nod
six	not
this	pop
tin	rob
wig	rot
	shot
	top

#23

short i	short u
big	bug
dig	but
dim	cub
fill	cup
fit	drum
hid	hut
him	must
hip	rug
his	run
it	shut
rich	slug
sick	tug
sip	up
six	us
tin	
win	

#24

short e	short o
best	box
den	drop
help	got
hen	hop
led	job
let	lot
net	mob
pen	mom
red	mop
send	not
sent	pond
ten	pot
went	rob
yes	rot
	sob
	stop

#25

short e	short u
bed	cub
beg	cup
elf	cut
fed	dug
jet	fun
leg	gum
men	hug
met	mud
red	nut
set	pup
ten	run
then	shut
when	sun
yes	tub
yet	up

#26

short o	short u
chop	cup
dot	fun
fox	gum
hot	much
mom	mud
not	mug
pop	must
pot	pup
rob	rug
rot	run
shop	shut
sob	sun
stop	tub
top	tug
	up
	us

#28

#27

short a	short e	short i	OUT OF SORTS
cat	den	him	coat
jam	held	lip	look
map	led	pig	
ran	leg	pink	
sad	let	pit	
sand	men	rip	
snap	red	ship	
tan	rest	sit	
wag	set	win	
		with	

short a	short e	short i	short o	OUT OF SORTS
lamp	bet	lift	cot	pup
man	help	rich	drop	run
raft	kept	rid	hot	
sad	met	six	job	
sag	sent	win	lost	
van	stem		sob	
	test		son	
	them		top	
	yet			

#29

short a	short e	short i	short o	short u

171

Answer Keys:

Vowel Sorts (#29-#35)

OUT OF SORTS

bath	belt	chin	top	bus	look
cap	get	dip	mom	dust	see
raft	pest	dish	soft	gum	
sand	test	milk	pond	hut	
swam	went	rich	lost	just	
	yes	wish		plum	

#30

short a	short e	short i	short o	short u	OUT OF SORTS
bath	bed	fish	clock	bump	seat
brag	best	fist	dock	gum	cute
camp	felt	fix	drop	rush	like
glad	went	gift	frog	shut	took
grab	wet	slid	stop	thud	
		twig			

#31

short a	short e	short i	short o	short u	OUT OF SORTS
ask	best	did	box	hunt	cars
cap	fed	his	clock	run	down
hand	left	inch	hot	shut	good
pan	next	rip	job	sun	right
swam	sent	will	not		row
	them				

#32

short a	short e	short i	short o	short u	OUT OF SORTS
can	dress	fill	fox	fun	bird
crab	get	him	got	hunt	boy
hat	help	sick	hop	hut	could
mat	leg	sink	lot	jump	farm
sand	well	trip	sock	up	like

#33

short a	short e	OUT OF SORTS
ask	bent	cut
camp	end	look
can	fell	my
dash	held	no
glad	help	sit
lap	left	
past	met	
plan	neck	
ran	nest	
sand	self	
sat	spent	
stand	went	
	yell	

#34

short a	short e	short i	OUT OF SORTS
act	bend	crib	book
damp	fed	dish	cry
glad	help	him	day
man	less	itch	great
sad	self	risk	these
that	sent	sink	
track	sled	spin	
	spend	stick	
	step	still	

#35

short a	short e	short i	short o	OUT OF SORTS
bad	bell	chill	box	boat
bath	lend	grin	clock	by
had	nest	his	fog	choose
map	sled	kiss	lot	foot
snack	stem	slid	rock	toy
wax	step	will	rod	
	them			

Answer Keys:

Vowel Sorts (#36-#44)

#36

short a	short e	short i	short o	short u	OUT OF SORTS
back	help	cliff	dot	mud	burn
camp	led	drink	fox	dump	cute
clap	red	hip	rod	rung	nose
scab	rent	slid	soft	truck	sky
track	stem	will	stop	spun	these

#37

short a	short e	short i	short o	short u	OUT OF SORTS
black	blend	dish	hot	club	boy
class	check	lit	shop	hug	could
crash	elf	ship	stop	jump	goose
hand	end	skip		scuff	me
mad	smell	wish		skunk	say
mash	spent				

#38

short a	short e	short i	short o	short u	OUT OF SORTS
band	egg	fill	block	bug	no
black	leg	fish	box	club	pie
lamp	mend	milk	lock	cut	say
snap	well	six	rock	plum	sheep
tan		will	trot	us	you
wag					

#39

short a	long a
ask	age
bath	cake
camp	grape
can	lane
cat	made
flag	pale
glad	plane
last	rake
mad	same
plant	shade
quack	shake
stand	take
swam	tale
than	whale
track	
trap	

#40

short a	long a
back	bake
bag	cane
cab	game
can	gate
fat	lake
had	late
ham	made
hand	make
has	name
man	plate
map	sale
pat	shade
rack	snake
rag	take
sad	
sand	

#41

short e	long e
bed	beak
beg	deep
fed	each
get	east
held	feel
left	feet
leg	green
let	meat
men	queen
neck	real
red	seal
step	seem
tell	sweet
tent	tree
	week
	year

#42

short e	long e
bend	bead
deck	clean
held	dear
help	hear
hen	heat
jet	jeep
kept	leave
led	mean
left	meet
men	need
send	seed
sled	steal
them	team
went	weak
wet	wheel

#43

short i	long i
big	cry
chin	dime
did	fine
dig	fire
gift	hide
him	life
hit	like
kid	mile
kiss	night
lift	nine
pin	ride
rib	sky
sick	tight
sink	time
sip	wise

#44

short i	long i
dish	find
fin	fine
hill	fire
hint	five
hit	hike
kick	like
lick	mind
miss	my
pig	nice
pink	nine
ship	pine
swim	right
tin	ripe
win	rise
	time
	tire

Answer Keys:

Vowel Sorts (#45–#52)

#45
short o	long o
box	boat
cross	coat
dog	cold
drop	go
frog	gold
hop	hole
job	home
knock	hope
lost	nose
moth	note
nod	roll
not	rope
top	rose
	soak
	toad
	toe
	woke

#46
short o	long o
boss	boat
clock	bone
cloth	broke
crop	croak
fox	dove
got	go
hog	mole
lost	no
mop	note
nod	pole
pond	rode
rob	rose
spot	smoke
stop	stole
	toast
	wore

#47
short u	long u
bump	blue
but	cube
duck	dude
fun	duke
gruff	fuse
gum	glue
hunt	June
hut	mule
jump	rude
lunch	rule
much	tube
mud	tune
pup	use
rug	
shut	
sung	
tub	

#48
short u	long u
brush	blue
bug	cute
bus	fluke
cub	flute
cup	fuse
cut	glue
dump	June
huff	mule
hunt	rule
junk	tube
mug	tune
must	use
plum	
run	
skull	
skunk	
thud	
trunk	

#49
short a	long a	long e
band	bake	beat
branch	blade	feed
clash	date	leaf
damp	pail	leave
flat	say	me
grab	skate	seem
plan	snake	sleep
stamp	train	squeak
wag	wade	sweep
	way	teach
		these

#50
short a	short e	long a	long e	long o
cab	bed	came	beet	bone
hat	best	gate	leaf	broke
map	neck	late	meat	coat
pack	pets	rain	sleep	road
sack	sell	save	steep	rope
trap	send	tape	these	stone

#51
short a	short e	short i
man	best	big
maps	men	did
that	ten	him
		six

long a	long e	long i	long o
chase	leaf	five	broke
plane	meal	pipe	hope
same	Pete	ride	pole
shade	sleep	ripe	smoke
whale	these	white	stone

#52
short a	short e	short i	short o
hat	bed	bit	not
mad	pet	rip	stop
pal	when	twin	top

long a	long e	long i	long o	long u
game	feel	bike	broke	cube
sale	meal	bride	hole	cute
stage	seal	kite	home	mule
wave	these			use

Answer Keys:

Vowel Sorts (#53-#60)

#53

short a	short e	short i	short o	short u
tap	hen	fin	pot	bus
that	pet	stick	rob	cub
wrap		this		cut
				fun

long a	long e	long I	long o	long u
grape	cheap	fine	code	cube
plate	clean	slice	home	mule
snake	these	smile	stroke	
	wheel		toast	

#54

short a	short e	short i	short o	short u
glad	bent	hit	mom	jug
rat	pen	thin	pop	pup
splash	set	swim	sob	

long a	long e	long i	long o	long u
brain	bead	drive	goal	cute
date	clean	white	moan	mule
flame	free	wipe	mope	
rate			toad	

#55

short a	short e	long a	long e
cash	best	came	feels
catch	fresh	date	green
fast	help	face	me
sand	send	jail	meat
snack	yet	made	need
than		plain	real
wrap		rain	seed
			sleep
			street
			teeth
			these

#56

short a	short e	short i	short o
fan	hens	kiss	clock
lamb	led	mix	knock
past	rent	stick	loss
that		win	not

long a	long e	long i	long o
sail	clean	fine	broke
snake	green	five	cone
stage	week	nine	note
wade		slice	rose

#57

short a	short e	short i	short o	short u	long a	long e	long i	long o
brat	check	miss	crop	run	date	cheek	bride	home
grand	nest	pick	fond	stung	fade	meet	time	road
stack	west	trip	rob		grape	these	wife	robe
		with			same			slope
					train			

#58

short a	short e	short i	short o	short u
glad	Fred	crib	frog	nuts
hat	melt	swim	spot	rung
hand	next	this		stuff

long a	long e	long i	long o	long u	OUT OF SORTS
cape	seem	drive	spoke	cube	proud
main	street	side	those	cute	threw
wait	these		toad	June	

#60

long a	long e	long i
brave	beach	dime
came	cheap	nine
may	green	pie
paint	sleep	side
plate	these	wise
wait		

long o	long u	OUT OF SORTS
hope	cube	cut
stove	cute	fog
stone	mule	pat
rose	use	set
woke		that

#61

#59

long a	long e	long i	long o	long u	OUT OF SORTS
gave	beat	fire	chose	cube	ask
make	creep	nice	cone	cute	clock
raise	deep	pipe	drove	fuse	help
snail	jeep	ride	poke	mule	must
train	queen	slide	stone	use	pill

Answer Keys:

Short Vowel Phonogram Sorts (#61-#66)

an	ap	ack	ank	ash	at	and	all
can	clap	back	bank	cash	brat	band	ball
fan	lap	black	drank	crash	cat	brand	call
man	map	crack	rank	dash	flat	grand	fall
pan	nap	pack	sank	flash	hat	hand	small
plan	rap	quack	tank	mash	mat	land	squall
ran	snap	shack	thank	slash	pat	stand	stall
tan	trap	snack		smash	that	strand	tall
than		stack		trash			wall
		track					

#62

#63

ack	ank	ap	an	ash	at	OUT OF SORTS
back	bank	cap	can	cash	brat	make
pack	tank	map	man	crash	chat	name
shack	thank	slap	plan	flash	flat	play
snack		snap	ran	rash	that	saw
tack		wrap		trash		

#64

ack	ank	an	ap	at	ash	OUT OF SORTS
back	bank	plan	lap	cat	crash	cake
shack	sank	scan	map	chat	dash	cane
tack	thank	span	snap	flat	mash	late
		than	tap	rat	rash	say
				that	smash	with
					trash	

#65

est	en	ell	et	ent	end
guest	hen	bell	get	bent	bend
nest	men	fell	let	cent	blend
rest	ten	shell	pet	lent	mend
test	then	smell	set	sent	send
west	when	yell		spent	spend
				tent	

#66

est	ell	en	et	ent	end	OUT OF SORTS
best	sell	hen	bet	bent	lend	do
chest	shell	men	get	dent	mend	itch
nest	spell	pen	let	sent	spend	nice
rest	tell	ten	set	tent		see
test	well	when				

#67

Answer Keys:

Short Vowel Phonogram Sorts (#67-#73)

ick	ill	in	ing	ink	ip	it
kick	chill	chin	spring	drink	hip	bit
pick	fill	pin	swing	pink	ship	lit
stick	pill	skin	thing	sink	sip	pit
thick	spill	thin	wing	think	tip	sit
	still	win				

#68

ick	ill	in	ing	ink	ip	it	OUT OF SORTS
quick	chill	chin	king	blink	sip	fit	kite
sick	spill	spin	string	pink	skip	hit	make
stick	will	thin	swing	think	trip	knit	pot
thick		twin	thing	wink		quit	so

#69

ock	op	ot	og	ock	op	ot	og	OUT OF SORTS
block	chop	dot	dog	block	chop	dot	dog	ice
clock	crop	got	fog	clock	hop	got	fog	make
dock	drop	hot	frog	dock	mop	knot	frog	told
knock	flop	knot	hog	knock	pop	lot	jog	use
rock	mop	not	jog	lock	shop	shot	log	
shock	shop	pot	log	rock	stop	spot	smog	
sock	stop	spot	smog	shock				
stock		trot		stock				

#70 **#71**

uck	ug	ump	unk	uck	ug	ump	unk	OUT OF SORTS
cluck	drug	bump	bunk	cluck	bug	bump	bunk	at
duck	hug	jump	chunk	duck	drug	dump	chunk	go
luck	lug	lump	dunk	luck	mug	lump	dunk	may
struck	mug	plump	hunk	stuck	plug	plump	junk	the
stuck	plug	pump	junk	truck	slug	pump	skunk	
truck	shrug	slump	skunk	tuck	snug	slump	sunk	
	slug	stump	sunk			stump	trunk	
	snug	thump	trunk					

#72 **#73**

ank	ink	unk
bank	blink	bunk
crank	clink	chunk
drank	link	drunk
plank	mink	dunk
prank	pink	hunk
rank	rink	junk
sank	sink	punk
spank	stink	skunk
tank	think	sunk
thank	wink	trunk

#74

Answer Keys:

Blend Sorts (#74–#80)

#75

bl	cl	fl
blank	clam	flat
blend	clip	flesh
blink	club	fling
block	clump	flip
		floor

gl	pl	sl		OUT OF SORTS
glad	plan	slab		cut
Glenn	plant	slam		its
glob	plug	slap		late
glum	plum	sled		went
		slept		

#76

br	cr	dr	fr
brag	crash	drag	free
brat	crib	drank	frog
brim	crush	drift	from
bring	crust	drum	front

gr	pr	tr	OUT OF SORTS
grass	print	trap	clock
green	prop	trip	jump
grin	prom	trot	pop
grip		trunk	

#77

bl	cl	fl	br	cr	fr	OUT OF SORTS
blank	clam	flag	brag	crab	free	bent
blast	clap	flat	brat	crash	friend	can
blend	clip	flip	brim	crib	frog	read
blink	cloth	flush	bring	crop	from	was
			brush		frost	

#78

gl	pl	sl	gr	dr	pr	tr	OUT OF SORTS
glad	plan	sled	grand	drag	print	trap	book
gland	plug	slept	grin	drip	prod	trim	cat
glass	plum	slid	grunt	drop	prop	trunk	house
glob		slot		drum	proud	trust	
glum							

#79

sc	sk	sm	sn	sp	st	sw	OUT OF SORTS
scab	skate	small	snap	spank	stand	sweet	cup
scalp	skid	smell	snip	spent	stem	swift	hats
scan	skin	smog	snug	spin	stop	swim	lake
scar	skip			spot	stunt	swing	some

#80

sc	sk	sm	sn	OUT OF SORTS
scab	skid	small	snag	sat
scales	skill	smash	snail	seat
scalp	skim	smell	snake	sit
scan	skin	smile	snap	some
	skip	smog	snip	sure
	skirt	smoke	snug	
	skit	smug		
	skunk			

#81

sn	sp	st	sw	OUT OF SORTS
snag	spark	stack	swam	sale
snake	speak	steep	swamp	same
snap	spent	step	swap	sent
sneak	spill	still	sweep	sing
snip	spin	sting	swell	sunk
snore	spy	stir	swift	
		stock		

Answer Keys:

Digraph Sorts (#81-#87)

ch	sh	OUT OF SORTS
chair	shark	cat
chart	sharp	cut
chat	shed	sail
cheap	sheep	sit
check	shell	
cheese	shin	
cherry	shine	
chest	ship	
chew	shoe	
child	shoot	
chin	shout	
chip	shut	
chop	shy	

#82

wh	th	OUT OF SORTS
whack	than	tent
whale	thank	toe
what	that	was
wheat	the	went
wheel	their	
when	them	
where	then	
which	these	
while	they	
whip	thin	
whistle	think	
white	this	
why	those	

#83

ch	sh	th	wh
chat	shed	than	what
chest	shelf	that	wheel
chick	shell	them	when
chimp	shop	they	which
chin	short	thing	while
chop	shot	this	whip
chunk	should	those	why
	shut	thump	

#84

ch	sh	th	wh
chat	shark	thank	whale
cheap	she	that	what
check	sheep	thick	wheat
cherry	shell	thin	when
child	ship	thing	where
chill	short	this	while
chose	should	thorn	why
chunk	shut		

#85

ch	sh	th	wh	OUT OF SORTS
cheat	shade	than	whale	cats
cheer	shark	that	wham	sits
chest	shop	thick	what	tub
chew	short	third	wheel	was
child	shout	this	when	
chomp	shut	thumb	whine	
chop			white	

#86

___ch	___sh	___th
beach	brush	booth
bench	bush	math
each	cash	moth
inch	dish	north
itch	leash	path
lunch	push	sixth
much	rush	south
ranch	trash	tooth
such	wash	with
teach	wish	worth

#87

ch___	sh___	th___	___ch	___sh	___th
chain	shack	that	itch	bush	bath
cheap	share	thick	much	crash	both
chest	shell	think	such	dish	path
chick	shout	thorn		push	sixth
chin	shy	thumb		smash	tooth
				wash	with

179

Answer Keys:

Plural and Ending Sorts (#88–#93)

#88

s	es
boys	brushes
cats	catches
cups	dresses
cuts	fishes
girls	glasses
mats	itches
nets	lashes
paths	latches
pens	mashes
pets	matches
pigs	passes
pins	patches
pups	wishes
shells	witches
sons	
wigs	

#89

s	es	ing
beeps	dashes	farming
boots	dishes	filling
chips	dresses	fishing
clocks	fishes	jumping
dogs	glasses	looking
ducks	hatches	marching
frogs	messes	rocking
reads	passes	seeing
socks	witches	selling
weeks		sleeping
		ticking

#90

ing	ed	OUT OF SORTS
cheering	acted	dress
coloring	backed	first
forming	chewed	sees
going	covered	
jumping	greeted	
laughing	guessed	
leaking	painted	
peeling	rained	
pinching	rowed	
reading	slowed	
seeing	spelled	
singing	thanked	
thinking	wanted	
walking		

#91

ed	ing	doubled final consonant + ed	doubled final consonant + ing
drifted	cooling	batted	batting
helped	crashing	chopped	cutting
packed	going	dotted	dragging
raked	melting	flagged	flopping
waited	nesting	jammed	lapping
wished	ringing	padded	patting
	spending	skipped	running
	talking	stopped	spinning

#92

singular nouns	plural nouns
cow	birds
desk	boxes
frog	bugs
gift	bushes
hat	dogs
hole	dots
letter	jars
lid	kisses
net	lunches
shark	planes
star	plates
tack	pools
tent	rocks
wagon	ropes
	turtles
	waves

#93

singular nouns	plural nouns
baby	babies
bus	children
child	clowns
*deer	*deer
goose	feet
hour	fishes
lemon	geese
lion	men
man	mice
*moose	*moose
mouse	radios
*sheep	seals
story	*sheep
tooth	teeth
woman	toys

* These words are repeated because they can be categorized as both singular and plural nouns.

#94

contractions	not contrac-

180

Answer Keys:

Contractions and Compound Words (#94–#98)

tions

aren't	are
can't	cannot
didn't	could
doesn't	did
don't	has
hadn't	have
hasn't	is
haven't	may
I'm	not
I've	should
isn't	they
it's	what
let's	
she's	
they're	
we'll	
we've	
won't	

#95

compound	not compound
airport	bike
bedroom	boy
cannot	girls
cookbook	jumping
daytime	key
doorbell	looked
football	paintingindoor
playing	inside sees
into	skipping
jellyfish	teeth
myself	them
seashell	
snowball	
someone	
suntan	
today	
tugboat	

#96

compound	not compound
anyone	boxes
backyard	brushes
bullfrog	chairs
butterfly	dresses
cannot	farmer
cowboy	horse
cupcake	house
goldfish	lakes
hilltop	mother
outfit	pillow
sailboat	sunny
seagull	tables
snowman	trees
somehow	water
without	wind

#97

contractions	compound words
can't	baseball
didn't	cannot
doesn't	everyone
hadn't	flashlight
I'll	herself
I've	homesick
isn't	indoor
it's	inside
she'll	into
they've	itself
we'll	seashell
what's	snowman
won't	sunshine
wouldn't	wheelchair
you've	without

#98

contractions	compound words	OUT OF SORTS
can't	anyone	runs
doesn't	crosswalk	seeing
don't	daytime	sit
hadn't	dugout	wrote
haven't	hilltop	
I'll	homemade	
isn't	into	
let's	nobody	
there's	outside	
what's	seesaw	
who's	softball	
you've	sunrise	
	teammate	
	tryout	

#99

ail   ain   ake   ale

Answer Keys:

Long Vowel Phonogram Sorts (#99–#105)

bail	brain	brake	bale	blame	crate	gray
fail	chain	cake	male	came	date	hay
hail	main	fake	pale	fame	fate	jay
jail	pain	lake	sale	flame	gate	may
pail	rain	quake	scale	frame	hate	pray
rail	stain	snake	tale	game	late	slay
snail	strain	stake	whale	lame	plate	spray
trail		take		name	rate	stay
#100				same	skate	stray
ame	**ate**	**ay**		tame	state	tray
				#101		
					ail	**ain**	**ake**

ale	**ame**	**ate**	**ay**			
frail	chain	flake	scale	blame	crate	gray
pail	main	quake	stale	flame	plate	spray
quail	plain	shake	tale	game	skate	stay
snail	Spain	snake	whale	name		stray
trail	stain			shame		

#102

ail	**ain**	**ake**	**ale**	**ame**	**ate**	**ay**
frail	brain	flake	sale	blame	crate	gray
jail	plain	sake	scale	frame	gate	pray
mail	sprain	shake	stale	lame	late	stay
nail	stain		whale	shame	plate	sway
sail				tame	skate	

#103

eat	**eek**	**eed**	**eep**	**een**	**eel**	**eeze**	**ear**	**eak**	**eet**
beat	cheek	bleed	beep	green	feel	breeze	clear	beak	beet
cleat	creek	feed	deep	queen	heel	freeze	dear	creak	feet
heat	Greek	need	sleep	screen	kneel	sneeze	fear	leak	greet
neat	peek	seed	steep	seen	peel	squeeze	hear	peak	meet
treat	reek	speed	sweep	sheen	steel	tweeze	smear	sneak	sheet
wheat	week	weed	weep	teen	wheel	wheeze	spear	speak	sleet
#104					**#105**				

east	**eal**	**ead**	**eap**	**ee**	**eave**	**eech**
beast	deal	bead	cheap	bee	heave	leech
feast	heal	knead	heap	fee	leave	screech
least	meal	lead	leap	flee	weave	speech
yeast	real	plead	reap	knee		
	squeal	read		see		
	steal					

#106

Answer Keys:

Long Vowel Phonogram Sorts (#106–#1112)

ice	ide	ight	ine	ile	ime	ipe	ite	ive	ike
dice	bride	bright	fine	file	chime	gripe	bite	dive	like
mice	glide	flight	line	mile	crime	ripe	quite	drive	Mike
nice	pride	fright	mine	pile	grime	stripe	white	five	pike
price	ride	knight	nine	vile	lime	swipe	write	strive	spike
slice	side	light	shine	while	mime	wipe		thrive	strike
spice	slide	right	spine		slime				
twice	stride	slight	swine	#108					
	tide		whine						
#107									

ide	ime	ine		oke	ore	oat	ode	old	one
bride	chime	nine		broke	chore	boat	code	cold	bone
glide	crime	pine		choke	core	coat	mode	gold	cone
hide	dime	shine		smoke	more	float	rode	hold	phone
pride	lime	spine		spoke	pore	goat	strode	scold	stone
slide	slime	vine		stroke	snore	throat		told	
tide	time	whine		yoke	store				

ipe	ive	ike		#110					
ripe	dive	bike		ope	ow	ote	ove	ome	ose
stripe	drive	like		cope	blow	note	clove	chrome	chose
swipe	hive	strike		hope	crow	vote	cove	dome	close
wipe	strive			mope	know	wrote	grove	gnome	nose
	thrive			rope	low		stove	home	pose
#109				scope	slow		wove	Rome	those
				slope	snow				
				#111					

ose	ope	one	oat	oke
chose	cope	bone	bloat	choke
hose	hope	cone	boat	joke
nose	mope	lone	float	poke
pose	rope	phone	goat	smoke
prose	scope	shone	moat	spoke
rose	slope	zone	throat	

#112

ue	ule	ume	une	use	ute	ube
blue	mule	fume	June	abuse	brute	cube
clue	rule	plume	prune	fuse	chute	tube
due	yule	spume	tune	muse	cute	
flue				use	flute	
glue					jute	
hue					lute	
sue					mute	
true						
#113						

Answer Keys:

R-Controlled Vowel Sorts (#113-#117)

er	ir	ur
clerk	bird	church
fern	dirt	curb
germ	fir	curl
jerk	firm	curve
nerve	first	hurt
perch	flirt	nurse
stern	shirt	purse
swerve	skirt	spurt
term	stir	surf
verse	thirst	turn

#114

ar	or
barge	born
card	cork
cart	cord
carve	fort
charm	forth
chart	horse
dark	north
harm	porch
harp	pork
large	port
march	short
park	sport
part	storm
shark	torch
start	worn

#115

ar	or
arm	born
bark	corn
barn	for
card	fork
cart	form
dark	horn
far	lord
farm	more
march	north
mark	ore
park	port
sharp	shore
tar	short
yard	sore
yarn	torn

#116

ar	er	ir	ur	or
carve	fern	bird	blur	cord
harm	nerve	birth	blurt	force
large	perk	chirp	burst	horse
lark	serve	firm	curve	north
march	term	skirt	nurse	sport
shark	verse	swirl	turn	thorn

#117

ar	ir	er	ur	or	OUT OF SORTS
barb	firm	clerk	blur	born	bear
harm	quirk	fern	burn	gorge	fire
mark	shirt	perch	churn	porch	here
scarf	squirt	stern	curl	storm	
sharp	third	term	nurse		
snarl		verse			

#118

Answer Keys:

Long Vowel Pattern Sorts (#118-#119)

ai	ay	ei
bait	clay	eight
faith	gray	eighth
frail	may	freight
grain	play	neigh
maid	ray	rein
paint	slay	sleigh
plain	spray	veil
quaint	stray	vein
strait	sway	weight
trail	tray	
waist		

#119

ai	ay	ei	OUT OF SORTS
paint	clay	eight	chose
praise	gray	freight	mat
quaint	pay	neigh	pet
saint	play	rein	want
snail	stray	sleigh	
sprain	sway	veil	
straight	tray	vein	
trail	way	weigh	
waist		weight	

#120

Answer Keys:

Long Vowel Pattern Sorts (#120–#127)

ee	ea	e	ie
beef	beach	be	field
cheese	flea	he	grief
green	leash	me	niece
kneel	peace	she	piece
seem	seal	we	shield
street	squeak		shriek
three	stream		thief
week	weave		
weep	wheat		

#121

ee	ea	ie	e	OUT OF SORTS
greet	feast	field	he	fed
queen	leak	piece	me	men
sleet	least	shriek	she	set
sleeve	sneak	siege	we	went
speech	speak	thief		
teeth	stream	yield		
weed	tea			
wheel	teach			

#122

igh	___y	i with 2 consonants
bright	cry	bind
fight	dry	blind
high	fly	child
knight	fry	climb
light	my	find
night	sky	grind
right	sly	kind
sigh	spry	rind
sight	spy	sign
thigh	try	wild

#123

igh	i with 2 consonants	___y	OUT OF SORTS
bright	child	cry	hid
flight	climb	fly	its
high	find	my	may
might	grind	pry	sit
night	kind	shy	
sign	mild	sky	
slight	wild	spry	
thigh		spy	
tight		try	
		why	

#124

oa	o with 2 consonants	ow
coal	bolt	bowl
coat	both	flown
groan	cold	grow
loaf	comb	growth
loan	ghost	know
moat	host	known
roach	jolt	own
road	poll	shown
soak	post	
toad	roll	
	sold	
	stroll	

#125

oa	o with 2 consonants	ow	OUT OF SORTS
croak	both	blown	cot
goat	fold	flown	log
load	folk	growth	mob
loan	ghost	know	mop
oath	hold	own	
road	host	show	
roast	post	snow	
soak	roll	throw	
soap		thrown	

#126

ue	ui	u_e
blue	bruise	brute
clue	cruise	chute
cue	fruit	crude
due	juice	dude
flue	suit	duke
glue		fume
hue		June
rue		plume
sue		prune
true		rude
		rule
		spruce
		truce
		tube
		tune

#127

ue	ui	u_e	OUT OF SORTS
blue	bruise	crude	burn
clue	cruise	dude	full
cue	fruit	duke	jump
due	juice	dune	pup
flue	suit	flute	put
glue		fume	
hue		June	
sue		plume	
		rule	
		tube	
		tune	
		yule	

#128

Answer Keys:

Vowel Diphthongs (#128-#134)

ea	ew	oo (moo)	oo (book)	oy	oi	ow (cow)	ow (show)	ou	ow
bread	blew	bloom	brook	boy	boil	brow	blow	bound	brown
breath	brew	coop	cook	boys	boils	brown	crow	cloud	clown
dead	crew	fool	crook	coy	broil	clown	flow	count	cow
deaf	dew	goof	good	joy	coil	crown	glow	doubt	down
death	drew	hoot	hood	joys	coin	down	grow	found	drown
dread	few	mood	hoof	ploy	coins	fowl	know	grouch	growl
feather	flew	moon	look	Roy	foil	growl	known	ground	how
heather	knew	noon	shook	soy	groin	how	low	loud	now
lead	new	proof	stood	toy	hoist	howl	mow	mound	owl
meant	screw	room	took	toys	join	owl	row	pouch	plow
spread	shrew	roost	wood		joint	plow	show	proud	scowl
stealth	shrewd	school			joist	prowl	slow	round	town
sweat	stew	scoot			moist	scowl	snow	scout	vow
thread	threw	smooth			oil	town	stow	sound	wow
tread		spoon			point	wow	tow	south	
wealth		troop			points	#132		sprout	
#129		wool			soil			#133	
		zoo			spoil				
		zoom			toil				
					void				
au	aw	#130		#131					
caught	claw								
cause	crawl								
fault	dawn								
fraud	draw								
gaudy	drawn								
gauze	gnaw								
haul	hawk								
haunch	jaw								
haunt	lawn								
jaunt	paw								
launch	raw								
pause	saw								
taught	shawl								
vault	squawk								
	straw								
#134	thaw								

Answer Keys:

Triple Blends and Digraphs (#135-#136)

scr	shr	spl	spr	squ	str	thr
screen	shrank	splash	sprain	squad	straight	thread
script	shriek	split	sprang	squeal	strap	throat
scroll	shrill	splotch	spring	squid	stream	throw
scrunch	shrimp	splurge	sprint	squint	stress	thrust
	shrug			squirt		

#136

scr	shr	spl	spr	squ	str	thr
scram	shrank	splash	sprang	squeal	stray	threat
scribe	shred	splint	spread	squid	stream	thrill
scrimp	shroud	split	sprout	squint	stride	thrive
script	shrunk	splurge		squirt	strike	throne
scroll					stripe	thrush

#137

au	aw	al
caught	crawl	chalk
fault	draw	false
fraud	gnaw	hall
gauze	hawk	halt
haul	lawn	malt
haunt	paw	salt
launch	saw	scald
taught	sprawl	small
vault	yawn	stalk
		talk
		walk
		waltz

#135

Answer Keys:

Sound-Alike Endings (#137-#142)

___ck	___ke	___k
check	choke	beak
crack	fake	desk
dock	flake	milk
kick	lake	park
quack	like	pork
stick	make	skunk
tack	quake	sleek
thick	spoke	sneak
track	take	week
truck	woke	wink

#138

___ck	___ke	___k
block	bike	bark
brick	flake	book
click	hike	junk
deck	joke	leak
knock	make	milk
pack	rake	pork
quick	shake	shook
sick	smoke	sleek
stick	spoke	stalk
stock	wake	
stuck		

#139

___ck	___ke	___k
black	bake	cheek
deck	broke	croak
lick	fake	dark
luck	flake	fork
neck	hike	sank
smack	like	slack
struck	poke	sneak
stuck	smoke	spark
track	spoke	weak
wreck	strike	week

#140

___ch	___tch	___ch	___tch	___ge	___dge
bench	batch	beach	batch	cage	badge
branch	catch	bench	blotch	change	bridge
church	clutch	branch	catch	charge	budge
crunch	crutch	church	ditch	fringe	dodge
gulch	ditch	crunch	fetch	gouge	edge
lunch	fetch	drench	itch	hinge	fudge
march	latch	hunch	hitch	huge	hedge
munch	match	lunch	latch	large	judge
peach	patch	munch	scratch	page	ledge
pouch	pitch	pinch	sketch	plunge	lodge
punch	scratch	porch	snatch	rage	nudge
reach	sketch	reach	stitch	range	pledge
teach	stitch	scorch	switch	sage	ridge
torch	switch	search	watch	stage	trudge
	watch	teach	witch	stooge	wedge
	witch				

#141   **#142**   **#143**

Answer Keys:

Silent Consonants (#143)

gn___	kn___	wr___	___mb
gnarl	knack	wrap	bomb
gnash	knead	wreath	comb
gnat	knee	wreck	crumb
gnaw	kneel	wring	dumb
gnome	knelt	wrist	lamb
gnu	knight	write	limb
	knob	wrong	thumb
	knot	wrote	tomb

#144

Answer Keys:

Sounds of the "ed" Ending (#144-#145)

___ed (dated)	___d (tried)	___t (mixed)
lasted	boiled	asked
melted	cleaned	bumped
needed	combed	crushed
planted	grabbed	fished
rented	joined	passed
roasted	rained	picked
squirted	rolled	rushed
started	sailed	splashed
twisted	smiled	stamped
	snowed	walked
		worked

#145

___ed (dated)	___d (tried)	___t (mixed)
aimed	asked	acted
batted	crowed	baked
melted	groaned	coached
parted	mailed	crushed
shifted	rolled	fished
treated	seemed	missed
trusted	showed	mixed
waited	trailed	picked
wilted	yelled	pushed
		skipped
		splashed
		winked

#146

Answer Keys:

Fun Sorts—Word Meaning (#146-#151)

number words	color words
eight	black
eleven	blue
five	brown
four	gray
nine	green
ninety	navy
one	orange
seven	pink
seventy	purple
six	red
ten	tan
thirteen	teal
thousand	violet
three	white
twelve	yellow
#147	

farm animals	zoo animals
calf	alligator
cat	bear
chicken	crocodile
chick	elephant
cow	giraffe
dog	gorilla
horse	hippo
kitten	hyena
lamb	koala
pig	lion
piglet	monkey
pony	panda
puppy	python
rooster	tiger
sheep	zebra
#148	

land vehicles	water vehicles	air vehicles
bike	canoe	airplane
bus	ferryboat	balloon
cab	jet ski	biplane
car	rowboat	blimp
motorcycle	sailboat	helicopter
roller skates	ship	jet
skateboard	submarine	rocket
tractor	surfboard	
trailer	tugboat	
train	water skis	
tricycle		
truck		
wagon		
#149		

has wheels	does not have wheels
bike	book
bus	cow
cab	cup
car	dog
jeep	flower
jet	glass
plane	horse
roller skates	jar
skateboard	paper
taxi	pen
tractor	pig
train	plate
tricycle	pots
truck	shoes
wagon	table
#150	

days of the week	months of the year	time words
Sunday	January	before
Monday	February	calendar
Tuesday	March	dates
Wednesday	April	months
Thursday	May	morning
Friday	June	today
Saturday	July	tomorrow
	August	week
	September	weekly
	October	year
	November	yesterday
	December	
#151		

living things	non-living things
bird	ball
bug	bike
cat	book
cow	chair
dog	cloud
fish	door
flowers	dress
kitten	flag
mouse	glass
parrot	hat
pig	pen
puppy	picture
rabbit	room
snake	table
trees	window
	#152

188

Answer Keys:

Fun Sorts—Word Meaning (#152-#155)

mothers	babies	city words	country words
bear	calf	airport	barn
cat	chick	banks	chickens
cow	cub	city buses	corn fields
dog	duckling	concrete	cows
duck	eaglet	crowds	crops
eagle	fingerling	escalators	farmer
frog	foal	freeway	haystacks
goat	gosling	factories	horses
goose	kid	malls	pasture
hen	kitten	neon sign	pigs
horse	nestling	skyscrapers	plow
owl	owlet	stadium	sheep
pig	piglet	subway	silo
robin	puppy	taxi	tractor
salmon	tadpole	traffic	
		trolley	

#153   **#154**

water words	land words	summer words	winter words
bay	canyon	baseball	blizzard
bayou	cliff	beach	freezing
creek	continent	fan	frigid
gulf	desert	hot	frosty
lake	dunes	picnics	gloves
ocean	grassland	sandcastles	ice-skating
pond	hill	scuba	icicles
puddle	island	sunburn	icy
raindrop	mountain	sunny	mittens
rapids	peninsula	suntan	sleet
river	plain	surfing	snowfall
sea	prairie	swimming	snowman
stream	shore	warm	snowshoes
tide		watermelon	toboggan
waterfall		water-ski	wind-chill
waves			

#155

Made in the USA
Lexington, KY
22 August 2010